Kai

Gets A Forever Home

Ashley Farasopoulos Brooks

ISBN 978-1-64416-679-6 (hardcover)
ISBN 978-1-64416-678-9 (digital)

Christian Faith Publishing, Inc.
832 Park Avenue
Meadville, PA 16335
www.christianfaithpublishing.com

With Illustrations by Suzanne Teixeira

Printed in the United States of America

My name is Kai. I was born with one eye, but I don't know any different.

I once had a family, but they didn't want me anymore, so they left me at the shelter.

I was very lonely and scared. I just wanted to be loved. I went from one shelter to another, and finally, there was one person who wanted to adopt me. They also changed their mind. I felt really sad. It must have been because I was different.

One day a kind man decided I really needed someone to love me. He found a lady who had always wanted a dog, so he decided to have her meet me to see if we got along.

3

I remember the moment the lady walked in the door. She walked over to me and started crying. She wondered how anyone could leave me. It was love at first sight. She picked me up, and I couldn't stop licking her. She said having one eye made me special.

I remember sitting on her lap, and
we both had very big smiles! I
couldn't wait to go home with her.
I think she felt the same way too.

Since I have been with my Mom, we have gone on many adventures together.

Our first trip we were in the car for a very long time. We were going to spend time with family for Christmas. I was so excited. I remember being in the car with all kinds of boxes and presents.

When we arrived, everyone was so happy to meet me. I got lots of hugs and kisses.

I got to go to the ocean for the first time! I loved running on the sand but didn't like getting splashed by a wave at all! I don't like getting wet!

I got to see the sea lions on the pier. They were very noisy. I didn't know what to make of their loud and strange barking.

I got to go kayaking! I have my very own life vest, and it even has a handle. Safety first, my Mom always says. I like to stand in the boat close to my Mom's lap. I enjoy smelling the ocean breeze and feeling the warm sun.

One of my favorite things to do is sunbathe on the patio.

One of my biggest adventures was going on an airplane to be in my Mom's wedding.

There was a lot of hustle and bustle going on during the wedding. All I cared about was being with my Mom.

14

When my Mom married my Dad, I felt safe with my new family.

15

I know some people think I look different, and maybe I do, but that's what makes me special. There is only one *you*! The right people will love and accept you no matter what, just like my family.

About the Author

Ashley Farasopoulos Brooks has always loved writing, even as a small child. This is her first published work. She is very passionate about animals, animal welfare, and supports several farm sanctuaries that carry out this tireless mission on a daily basis. A portion of the proceeds of this book will be donated to several of these organizations.

Ashley has a very special place in her heart for animals that are overlooked by the typical person. She finds their differences very endearing. This book was written in hopes that more animals will find forever homes, just like Kai.

Ashley lives in Los Angeles, California, with her husband and rescue dog Kai, the subject of the book, along with their new baby girl.

The Brooks Family

CPSIA information can be obtained at www.ICGtesting.com
Printed in the USA
BVIW120931190220
572427BV00003B/2